CONTENTS

RESPECT PARENTING

A behavioral parenting program

Robin Fann Fitzgerald

Robin Fitzgerald

PREFACE

Parenting is not for the weak at heart!

My first week of parenting was very memorable. After my son's birth, we spent three delightful days with the attentive nurses meeting our needs. They fed our baby when I was tired, diapered him when I needed to rest, and provided emotional support during the sleepless nights. In the safe confines of the hospital, parenting looked easy.

That all changed, however, as soon as we left the hospital doors. Immediately after getting in the car for the trip home, I looked at my husband and asked two questions. The first question was, "Are they really going to let us take him home?" The second question was, "Do they realize that we have absolutely no idea what we are doing?"

I remember that it amazed me that competent health professionals would consider it plausible to release a sweet baby to two parents who had absolutely no clue what to do with him! At that point all that I wanted was a class, or at least written instructions to help us figure out what to do with our new bundle of joy.

Eventually, we figured out how to hold our son, feed him, diaper him, and stop his tears. However, with each new life stage, we have often been "in the dark" about how to navigate through the difficult waters.

Now, our boys are nearly grown; for the last eighteen years, we have managed to parent them without an instruction manual but with reliance on God and lots of prayer.

A parenting manual *would* have made things much easier. My husband and I could have used a guide to help us navigate the tantrums of toddlerhood and the whirlwind of the emotions of puberty. It would have been nice to have some help with stopping negative behaviors, backtalk, and willful disobedience.

My hope is that this parenting program will provide you with the guidance that my husband and I needed when our boys were young. It comes from a culmination of different ideas- from biblically based resources to my training as a Cognitive Behavioral Therapist. Proverbs says there is nothing new under the sun, and honestly there is not. Hopefully, this new guide will organize the old information in a way that is useful as you move through your parenting journey.

God bless!

Robin

CHAPTER ONE

God's Design for Parenting
"Our children are not our own."

Do you struggle with your child? Does your son rebel at home or at school? Does your daughter talk back instead of following through the first time with your requests?

You are not alone. After many years of working as a Cognitive Behavioral Therapist, I have seen many families experiencing the same problems.

In fact, I too, struggled with parenting. Early on, I read lots of books, yet, I never found the book I needed that would tell me specifically how to change my child's negative behavior. I can remember trying to prevent my two-year old from having meltdowns. I recall with agony how I inappropriately handled the behavior of my other child as he refused to do his homeschool work. I tried everything possible to convince my children to exhibit the behaviors that I desired. When those methods didn't work, I usually ended up yelling, fussing, or applying consequences that were totally inappropriate. I did things wrong... a lot.

After much prayer and study, I discovered there is a method to change your child's behavior. Anyone can apply the principles and when followed, you will see results. My goal in writing this book is to give you this information, the information that you need to consistently change your child's behavior.

Following years of study, what I have discovered is that behavioral change is fairly easy for the child. Unfortunately, the hard work towards changing your child's behavior begins with *you- the parent. You* must begin to implement parenting changes to achieve the behavior changes that you desire from your son or daughter.

This fact bothers people when they come to me for counseling. I can see it on their faces each time I begin to teach behavioral interventions to them - the *parents*, and not the child.

I want you to know that I understand that it is your *child* misbehaving. I realize that it is your *child* that needs to change; it is your *child* disrupting the house with negative behaviors. But, your child's behavior change begins with you.

In an imaginary world, you could drop your child off with a therapist for one hour and she could, in that one hour, transform your child's behavior. Unfortunately, that works only in imagination. Instead, it takes consistent, daily, even hourly practice for a child to change his behavior.

Have you ever tried to do an activity like playing an instrument or knitting? The first time that you try the activity, you are slow and clumsy. It takes a long time to finish the activity and in your mind the process is "cloudy" even after you progress through the stages. Only after you finish the activity and repeat the same procedure again and again can you produce the correct results.

I remember when I first started playing the piano without music. I would miss most of the notes. I would have to think how to form chords. I would have to break each song down into segments and play that segment over and over to get it right.

Now, however, after years of playing, I can sit down at the piano and play lots of songs with little effort. With practice, the act became easy.

To achieve behavioral change, when your child exhibits appropriate behaviors, something must be done to reinforce the postive behaviors. When your child exhibits negative behaviors, something must be done to extinguish the inappropriate actions. At the moment that the behaviors occur your child must be "caught," and a reinforcement given. For the behavioral change to be effective, the positive behaviors must be practiced over and over.

Unless a therapist lives at your home, he or she can't catch these acts of positive or negative behavior. As a result, your job as parent becomes very important. Cognitive Behavioral therapists "teach" you how to be a therapist; they teach you how to catch the positive behaviors to implement a positive consequence so that the behaviors will be repeated; they teach you how to catch the negative behaviors and reinforce so that negative behaviors will be extinguished. Cognitive Behavioral therapists teach *you* how to change your child's behavior. Using this book as a guide, you will be able to change your child's behaviors.

Some children seem to "get it right" the first time and you never need a book for instruction. Some children listen without questions; they try to please you; they don't want to break the rules. Some children seem to have an innate sense of how to obey.

There is, however, an equal number of kids who do not "get it right" without their parents intervening with behavioral strategies. This fact doesn't make them bad. Every child possesses a different personality, a gift from God.

Some of the children that God creates are naturally strong-willed; I believe it is in their DNA. Often, it takes more effort and training for them to produce the behavior that we desire.

I was a strong-willed child and am now a strong-willed adult. After years of struggling with my own strong- will, I can quickly identify and appreciate strong-willed children. In God's sense of humor, or as compensation to my parents, God allowed me to birth a strong-willed child. Although my strong-willed son requires additional effort, I know that he is going to do great things in the world because of his determination! Parenting the strong-willed child is not always easy, but it is important to remember that God has created your child perfectly for the work that He has for him.

When I think about my own formidable will and my son's, I like to think about the prophet Ezekiel in the Bible. In the book of Ezekiel, chapter 2, God told Ezekiel that He made him hard-headed so that he could minister to the hard-headed people to which he was called. God created your strong-willed child perfectly to accomplish great things for his kingdom. Using this book, you can channel your son or daughter's strong-will for good.

God gives us our children to raise. He knows our skills and abilities, so he places the perfect child in each family. He trusts us to do the hard work towards encouraging him or her to become what He intends in His kingdom.

Our Children Do Not Fully Belong to Us

Our children do not fully belong to us. God gives them to us for eighteen years to train so that they can become independent men and women who will advance his plan on earth. God's intended purpose, I believe, is that we become the hands and feet of Jesus. We raise these precious gifts from Him as Jesus would if he were walking with us today.

That idea sounds good, but when we get into day to day parenting, often, it is hard to see our children as anything but a reflection *of* and *on* us. We desire that they behave correctly because we see their behavior as direct evidence of our worth or at least of our skill at parenting. However, the children that God gives us are really individuals with their own souls. These souls will one day stand before God.

Each child that God gives us is unique with his or her own strengths and weaknesses. It is our job as parents to cultivate the strengths and work to extinguish the weaknesses.

Psychology says parents are "first gods." In other words, we get our idea about God from the way that our parents interact with us. Parents model characteristics of the Heavenly Father for their children.

Studies show that earthly fathers are specifically very important because they greatly impact a child's view of the Heavenly Father. A child who has a harsh demanding father might view God as harsh and demanding. A child that has a passive father might view God as absent and not caring. How we parent our children is vital because it influences the way that they view God and how they see His interaction with them.

So, what exactly does God expect from us in our job as parents?

I believe that we have at least three jobs when raising our children. First, we have a duty to become a facilitator to guide our children in God's path. Second, we have the job of demonstrating God's unconditional love. Third, we have the job of teaching our children obedience.

What does it mean to be a facilitator to our children?

Our first job as parents is to become a facilitator to guide our offspring towards God's path. We must provide our child with the correct resources to make good decisions as he or she navigates through life. We must also help our child to begin the work that God has called him or her to do and to find his or her place in God's Kingdom on earth. We must help our child find God and His perfect plan.

Our job as facilitator is perhaps the most important part of Christian parenting. It means being aware that our children have souls that will one day stand before God. It means doing everything in our power to ensure that we provide them the resources to know and love God.

What does it mean to demonstrate unconditional love?

Our second job as parents is to demonstrate God's unconditional love. Unconditional love is difficult. We, as parents, come into this parenting job with our own wounds.

Perhaps you were parented by people who could only show conditional love to you and now you have hurts that make it difficult for you to demonstrate unconditional love. Demonstrating God's unconditional love means that we demonstrate love even when our children are disobedient and even when they fail to measure up to our expectations or "miss the mark."

Thankfully, "unconditional love parenting" is the parenting style that our Heavenly Father uses as he parents us. The story of the Prodigal Son from the Bible is one of my favorite stories and is a perfect example of God's "unconditional love parenting." Many believe the story is about the rebellious son, however, I believe the story is really about the unconditional love of the father- a picture of the way that God loves us.

The Bible tells us that the son in the Prodigal Son story lived a riotous life. I'm sure that at times he upset his father and embarrassed him with his behavior. The son, as a strong-willed child, wanted to do everything his own way. Eventually, due to his bad choices, he ended up in the pig pen feeding pigs.

Even though his son had bad behavior, I believe that every day the father went outside and looked across the horizon searching for his son. Probably he woke up each morning with the thought "this will be the day in which my son comes home."

After a time, the son did come to his senses and decided to return to his father. On the glorious day of his return, the father ran to meet him with outstretched arms. It is interesting to note that the father did not heap condemnation on his son or remind him of the many problems that he had caused; instead, he restored him to his rightful position. He gave him a ring for his finger and a robe to wear. He had a celebration in his honor.

I love this story because it is a beautiful picture of the way that God loves and parents us. God does not wait to heap condemnation on us; his desire is to restore us when we stray.

The story also paints a picture of the way that God requires that we love the children that he has entrusted to us. At times they do the wrong thing and grieve our hearts, however we must identify their behaviors as wrong while providing them with unconditional love so that they can correctly understand God's love.

Providing unconditional love to your child means correctly labeling the behavior without labeling the child. Even though the Prodigal Son exhibited bad behavior, he was still the much loved, much adored son of his daddy. *He* was not bad, even if his behavior was not the best. Unconditional love means communicating to your child his worth, how much you love him, even when he does wrong.

What does it mean to teach obedience?

Our third role as parents is to teach our children obedience. The Lord requires that we have respect of him. As adults, when He speaks, we should listen and follow His will for our lives. Part of our job as parents is to teach our children how to obey. The learning process for obedience begins in the child's relationship with you, his parent.

Our children should obey us, but the idea of obedience leads us to the idea of grace. Often your child will not "get it right" the first time. If you think about your life as it relates to God, I bet there have been times when you haven't gotten obedience right.

Thankfully, God has been full of grace in my life. Instead of harshly punishing me when I am disobedient, usually, he gently nudges me in the right direction.

I am not suggesting that you let disobedience slide. That would reinforce negative behavior. However, I do believe that just as God gives us grace, we should give our children grace too. Usually I give my children several chances to "get it right." If they don't comply with my request the first time, I do not immediately punish with harsh consequences. Instead, I will give a second reminder and a choice- I let them choose to obey or choose the consequence.

Psychology has proven that positive consequences change behavior much quicker than negative. Any chance that you have at giving grace by reinforcing with something positive, do it! I have seen remarkable results in my practice with positive consequence parenting. Parents are always amazed at how quickly their children respond.

The RESPECT parenting program

As we parent we must realize that we are doing more than shaping behavior; we are training our children to become adults who love and understand God and have a desire to work for his kingdom. These ideas are the foundation in which we build our parenting program.

The RESPECT parenting program has seven aspects. You can remember the program by thinking of the word RESPECT, an acronym to help you remember the following steps:

R- Develop a **relationship**
E- Communicate clear **expectations**
S- Educate on **skills** to accomplish the correct behaviors
P- **Provide** options
E- **Encourage** and allow your child make decision

C- Give the **consequence**s

T- **Train** again if needed

In the following chapters, we will go over each part of the program. Don't be discouraged if you do not see immediate results. Sometimes things get worse before they get better. Be consistent and soon you will see positive changes.

Before we end this chapter, I would like to talk about a few parenting barriers. These barriers will sabotage the work you are doing towards behavior change.

Parenting Barriers: Things that will undermine your work

1. Mom and Dad not unified in their parenting of the child

One of the biggest problems that I see during therapy is when mom and dad are not "on the same page." Children are brilliant and when mom and dad are not unified, children capitalize on that fact and play one parent against the other. They do not do it to be malicious; however, it happens every time there is conflict or dis-unification in the family. To get the desired results from your children, parents must present a united front. If not, it will be almost impossible to change your child's behavior.

2. Parents modeling bad behavior but expecting different behaviors in kids.

Do as I say not as I do parenting does not work. The main place that your child is learning behavior is from you. Every day, every second, you model for your children how to be an adult. If you exhibit negative behaviors in your life but you are telling your child not to do those same behaviors, it will be almost impossible to change your child's behavior.

3. Getting into verbal or physical altercations with your child.

I tell my clients in counseling that when you begin to engage in arguments or fights with your child, your child has already won. You must maintain a calm atmosphere when dealing with him or her. At times altercations act as a positive reward for your child; altercations provide attention- even if it is negative attention. Take a time -out for yourself if you feel that things are spiraling out of control and then handle the situation when you are calm.

CHAPTER TWO

R- Work on the Relationship
7x7x7

When I do marriage counseling one of the first things that I ask is, "What fun things do you do together?" If the couple is having trouble, most of the time, they can't name any fun activities they still share.

Then, I ask them, "What did you do when you first started dating?" The couple usually tells me lots of things that they *used to* enjoy. Sometimes they say that they enjoyed biking together or going to the movies or the gym. Other couples tell me they enjoyed tennis, or dancing, or music.

Usually a couple begins to have trouble when they fail to nurture the relationship, when they stop spending quality time together. In marriage counseling, the first thing that I have them do is plan a date night to re-implement the activities that they enjoyed in the beginning of their relationship.

We live in a busy world and it is hard to make time to do everything that we need to do. Often, we are so busy *doing* that we forget to experience the world and the people in it. We might move from task to task without taking the time to nurture our connections with others. This becomes a major barrier in marriages and often is a problem in the relationships that we have with our kids.

The first part of RESPECT parenting is to work on the relationship between you and your child.

Take a minute and think about the time that you spend with your child. Quality time with your child should be time spent without triangulation. For example, it shouldn't be time that you spend with your children in front of a TV or electronic device; instead, it should be actual one on one time. Quality time with them should also be time spent doing something your child enjoys- not homework or classwork.

Many children feel loved based on the time that their parents spend with them. If we spend little to no time with our children, they do not feel our love, even when we love them dearly.

As mentioned earlier, our job as parents is to model God. For our kids to view God correctly and to communicate to them how important and valued they are to Him, we must spend time with them. We must let them know how important they are to us.

I realize that at this point you are probably thinking that I have this whole program backwards. Maybe you want to point out to me that *they* are doing *wrong* and need correction; so why am I talking about quality time?

Many behaviors can be corrected simply by using this chapter. When a child feels loved they are much more agreeable and willing to listen, communicate effectively, and work with you.

When a child feels unloved, or not heard, or neglected, they will often act out. School is difficult for some children. Being bullied or having few friends creates negative emotions. If our child's love tank is empty from the world, it will be difficult for him to have a good relationship at home. Sometimes our job as a parent is to be his number one supporter and to keep him feeling full of love.

I am encouraging you in this chapter to work on the relationship that you have with your child. I have a formula to help called 7x7x7. If you can remember this formula, you will be able to communicate to your son or daughter how much you love them in a way that he or she can understand.

7x7x7 for Relationships

My 7x7x7 formula is broken down into three sevens. The first seven stands for spending at least seven minutes of uninterrupted time with your child doing something he or she enjoys. The second seven stands for seven compliments or positive verbal consequences (which we will talk about later) that you give your child each day. The third group of sevens stands for seven acts of touch that you demonstrate towards your child per day. Remember 7x7x7 to keep your child feeling loved!

First seven- seven minutes of uninterrupted time doing something your child enjoys

The first 7 of 7x7x7 is 7 minutes of uninterrupted time with your child doing something he or she enjoys. Maybe you are thinking that seven minutes sounds like a small amount of time to give your child. However, when I look back on my time with my children, I realize rarely did I spend even seven minutes of one-on-one time with my kids.

I homeschooled and even though for many years I was

able to spend the whole day in the presence of my children, most days I did not meet the seven- minute goal. When they were young, I was busy trying to school them, cooking their meals, or cleaning the house. Rarely did I give them seven minutes of uninterrupted quality time doing something *they* enjoyed.

How about you? Consider your life with your child. How much uninterrupted time do you spend with your child doing something he or she enjoys each day?

If you already meet the seven-minute goal, you can check the first seven off. However, if you are not meeting the goal, plan to give your child seven minutes per day of quality time.

Second seven- seven compliments or seven verbal positive consequences

The second 7 of 7x7x7 is to give seven compliments to your child or seven verbal positive consequences. We will talk about verbal positive consequences later; they are important for shaping your child's behavior. Until we cover verbal positive consequences for shaping behavior, try to give your child seven compliments per day. Tell him how good he is at sports or praise him for a good day at school. If you "catch" her doing the right thing, praise her for her positive behavior.

Many children understand love from the words we give them. Make sure that you keep them feeling "full of love" by telling them the great things they are doing.

If you are having a difficult time finding things to compliment, think about the strengths that God has given your child. Write down the list and use those as your compliments. For example, you could say, "You are an awesome singer," or "I love the fact that you are kind to your grandmother" or "Thank you for picking up your clothes off the floor."

Third seven- seven acts of physical touch

The third 7 of the 7x7x**7** is to give seven acts of affection or physical touch each day. Studies show that people need physical touch to be emotionally healthy. Plus, some kids understand love from touch and without it, feel unloved.

One day your child will be a parent and will need to be able to provide affection to his or her child. If he has not had a model of appropriate affection, he will not understand how to display it to his family.

I grew up in a family that did not exhibit physical touch. As a result, physical touch is difficult for me. I work hard to offer enough touch to meet my children's needs.

My husband on the other hand grew up in a family that was very good at acts of affection. It comes naturally to him to hug our boys and rough-house them.

How about you? Did you grow up in an affectionate family? If so, it is probably easy for you to display affection to your child. If you are like me and were rarely hugged or touched, you might have a harder time.

In the third group of sevens, I ask you to give seven acts of touch or affection to your child. If you have difficulty in this area, you can use the suggestions below.

In addition, some of our children will say that they don't like physical acts of affection. If your child is one of these, you might try the physical touch examples with stars at the end of the list.

Physical touch:
Hugs

Snuggling
Kisses on the cheek
Tickle fun
**wrestling
**playing tag
** holding hands
** family sandwich / group hugs
** touches on the arm after positive comments
**arm wrestling
** thumb wars

My husband who is great at physical touch will often grab my boys and hold them in a wrestle-type hold. They will laugh and try to get away, but they love the physical play. He might also "play fight" (don't do this if you think that you might get angry or physically aggressive); he runs into them so that they will retaliate back. He teases them as he does it. They love this type of wrestle/ play. If you use this, keep it light and fun, don't let it escalate into something negative.

CHAPTER THREE

E- Clearly Explain Your Expectations

Have you ever worked at a job in which you were given a task to do but you were only given sketchy details about what was expected? If you've worked at a job like that, then you know how difficult it is to be successful without a clear and thorough explanation of the expectations.

Although children might initially seem opposed to expectations, psychology states that children feel more secure when they have rules and structure. Psychology also states that children need to know their proper place in the family. Even though children assert behaviors that indicate that they want to be the "top dog" in the family, studies show that this makes them feel insecure. Instead, children need to understand that they are under parental authority, with mom and dad at the top and them below.

The next part of RESPECT parenting ensures that you give your child clear specific information so that he or she can be successful at behavioral change. The **E** stands for: clearly **e**xplain your **expectations**. There are several places in which you can give specific expectations to make things easier for your child to be successful.

Family Meetings

Parents can clearly communicate their overall expectations for the child in a weekly or monthly family meeting. During the meetings, you discuss with your child the family plan that you have created. It is during this meeting that you clearly lay out the expectations that you have for your family values; you provide your children with your expectations concerning the way that they treat others and function in your family.

A family plan consists of your family values and might look like this.

In our family we:

1. Love and honor God
2. Respect others
3. Tell the truth
4. Don't talk back
5. Display kindness
6. Appropriately represent the family by making good choices
7. Listen

You can have a few points in your family plan that summarize your values, or you can have many specific parts. Some people use the Ten Commandments as a guide, while others choose to come up with the values on their own. Either way is fine; the important thing is that you clearly communicate what is expected in your family.

If your children are small, you might want to present a smaller family plan so that they are not overwhelmed with a big list of values. Try to group the behaviors into headings like: respect, kindness, peacefulness. Under each heading you can list the desired behaviors like "no hitting your brother" or "listening the first time." For older children or teenagers, you have more leeway to create a detailed family plan including your family expectations in many areas.

As you might have noticed, I am using the terms "values" and "behaviors" interchangeably. While there is in reality some difference, for our exercise we will consider "family values" the "behaviors" that you desire exhibited by your child.

In the next chapter we will talk about breaking each value or behavior into a specific skill set so that the value or behavior is easier understood and taught. A behavior differs from a skill, but a "family value" can be understood as a "behavior" that is learned or reinforced within a family.

Making a chart of family values allows children to see what is expected of them. Giving them input into the family decision making process helps them "buy into" the plan.

The family plan helps communicate the overall values of the family to your child. Once you create a family plan, you can refer to the plan as you communicate specific expectations.

Daily Expectations

Expectations should be given in the form of a family plan, but parents must also communicate expectations on a day to day basis. You must communicate your expectations not only about large family values, but you also must communicate expectations about daily behaviors.

When you communicate to your children what behaviors you would like to see, you must communicate clearly and specifically; use as many details as possible so that your child will understand exactly what you are expecting him or her to do. For example, you might say, "Please take out the trash and put it in the large trashcan outside. I need you to do it right now and to do it without fussing or grumbling. Remember we are working on listening and I need you to listen the first time."

Before a child goes into a new situation, you need to teach them or explain to them what is expected. People call this preventive teaching and it is necessary every time before your child enters a new situation. No child should be allowed to go into a new situation without knowing the expectations specifically and clearly. For example, you might say, "Remember, when you are at the party, I expect that you act respectful and kind to the people at the party. Remember to say please and thank you. Don't be on your phone at the table." Tell your child exactly how you expect him or her to act.

Also, use preventive teaching before situations in which your child has had problems in the past. Clearly break down the expectations that you have for your child. Do it when your child is NOT misbehaving or is NOT involved in anything else.

You might consider picking a family rule or behavior from your family plan each week and work on it as a family. For example, you might say, "This week we are working on respect which is on our family plan." During that week, you remind your child of the behaviors that you expect and provide him with teachable moments. If you notice disrespect occurring during your respect week, refer to the value on your family plan. Say, "This is what I'm talking about, we are working on respect this week, was that behavior respectful?"

During the explanation stage it is important to remain calm and realize that your child will probably not be able to achieve the behavior that you desire the first time. Learning new positive behaviors takes time and practice. We must give our children grace as we try to shape their behaviors.

The important thing to remember about "expectations" is you must overcommunicate! I can remember asking my son to do something when he was younger. I gave him a direct request and I felt as if I had communicated clearly. After a few minutes, however, it looked as if my son was willfully disobeying my request. Finally, I said, "Why are you disobeying me?" It was not until he answered, "I am trying to do it, but I don't understand what you want" that I realized that part of his "not listening" was that I was not communicating on his level.

Kids do not understand "adult talk." They cannot get the nuances and inferences that other adults might be able to understand. It is important to communicate to them much more information than you think necessary. Tell them clearly, specifically, and completely what behavior you are expecting. Tell them what the behavior looks like and how to accomplish the desired behavior. Verbally provide more information than you would normally give. Then, your child will have a better chance of producing the behavior you desire.

We have now covered the first two aspects of RESPECT parenting. The R stands for work on the relationship by using 7x7x7. The **E** reminds us to clearly **explain expectations.**

Robin Fitzgerald

Notes:

CHAPTER FOUR

S- Teach Skills to accomplish
desired behaviors

Have you ever tried to accomplish something difficult? If you have tried to accomplish a difficult goal, you know the best way to accomplish it is to break it into smaller parts.

My mom was a pianist who played beautifully by ear. When I was a child, she made it seem as if one day she sat down on the piano and God gifted her with the ability to play. My whole life I felt sad. Playing by ear seemed impossible, and I felt as if God had not gifted me in the same way.

As an adult, I decided I was going to learn to play the piano by ear. I bought a book that taught me the skills needed to play the piano. First, I learned how to form major chords and then minor chords; next I learned how to play seventh chords.

After I learned the skills of forming chords, I learned how to play some patterns on my left hands. Eventually I practiced putting my right hand together with my left hand. After learning the basic skills, I practiced, and practiced, and practiced.

Now, I can play most songs by ear. After lots of practice, I no longer must think about the individual skills; now, I play the piano without having to think about the parts.

To learn to play the piano, however, I had to divide the goal into manageable parts; I had to learn each individual skill. After I learned the skills, I put them together and was able to accomplish my goal- I could play the piano.

Behavior change works the same. To learn a desired behavior, the behavior must be broken into parts or skills. Each skill must be taught. Each behavior may contain four or five skills to help your child to accomplish the behavior.

For example, let's supposed that you want to teach your child the behavior of not talking back. To teach him or her that behavior, you would break the behavior into a set of skills. The skill set might look like this.

When someone asks you to do something you do not like, not talking back looks like this:
1. Look the person in the face
2. Maintain the correct facial expression
3. Acknowledge that you have heard what the person is telling you in a pleasing manner
4. Repeat back the request
5. Perform the behavior

Break specific behaviors down into skill sets. You should also break family values/ family plans into skill sets to teach the values or behaviors.

A multitude of behaviors can be taught by breaking down the behavior into skill sets. You can come up with your own skill sets. I have included some common behaviors and skill sets to get you started.

Obedience
- Look the person in the face
- Maintain the correct facial expression
- Acknowledge that you heard the person

- Repeat back the request
- Do the behavior
- Check back to ensure that you did the behavior correctly

Telling the truth
- Think about the answer to each question
- Before you answer, ensure that your answer is truthful
- Provide the truthful answer
- Determine the difference between a joke and a lie
- If you are joking say, "I'm joking" before you tell a joke.

Making good choices

- List your options
- Think about the consequences for each option
- Consider what your parents would like
- Consider what God would like
- Make the best decision

Listening
- Quit talking
- Look the person in the eyes
- Repeat back what you think the person is saying
- Clarify anything you don't understand
- Maintain the correct body posture
- Maintain the correct facial expression

Accept consequences
- Look the person in the eye
- Maintain correct face and body posture
- Don't interrupt
- Acknowledge you've heard by saying, "Yes I understand."
- Keep your body calm.
- Comply

Accepting criticism

- Look at the person
- Acknowledge that you have heard them
- Maintain correct body and facial expression
- Wait to discuss concerns until you have calmed down

Asking Permission
- Decide what it is you want to do
- Ask your mother or father or authority figure about your request in the form of a question
- Comply with the answer

Calming out of control emotions
- Count to ten
- Use deep breathing
- Keep calm voice and body
- Consider options
- Consider consequences
- Makes the right decision
- Calm down

Take a moment and think about the behaviors you would like to change in your child. Quickly list the behaviors and come up with the skills that you need to teach your child so that he or she can achieve the correct behavior.

As you teach the behavior, educate your child on the skill set. For example, if the desired behavior is "staying on task" say, "We are learning to stay on task. This is what I expect you to do. First you need to begin the task when asked. Then, you need to ask for help if you need it. I expect you to work quietly in your seat and not leave your room. I expect you to stay there until your task is complete. Do you have any questions about how to stay on task?" Wait for your child to respond. Then say, "Do you think that you can do this?" Wait for your child to respond. Finally, ask your child to repeat back the steps of the skill set. You might also consider listing the steps on paper and placing them in front of your child to help him remember.

Continue to use R- work on the relationship-7x7x7. Don't forget, E- explain your expectations. Now, focus on S- breaking down behaviors into a skill set.

Robin Fitzgerald

Notes:

CHAPTER FIVE

P-Provide Options

Hopefully after you clearly explain to your child your expectations and teach them the skill set to succeed in the behavior, your child will make the right decision towards the correct behavior. That is our goal, but unfortunately, this does not always happen.

There are times that you give your child a directive and they immediately listen and do what they are supposed to do. There are other times however, especially as you work on changing behaviors, when your child will refuse to do what you ask, or he or she may fail to do it correctly. There are two different possible outcomes- either your child does the right thing or your child refuses to do the right thing.

What do you do when your child does the right thing?

If your child immediately does the right thing, you can skip to the "C" chapter of this book. You do not need this step or the next step- move straight to the "consequence" section. Immediately following your child doing the right thing the first time, you should reward him with a positive consequence. You can learn more about positive consequences in the "C- Give a Consequence" chapter.

Studies show that positive consequences shape your child's behavior much quicker than negative. You should take every opportunity to give your child positive consequences. We will talk about the different types of consequences later. Until we get to the consequence section, you can use verbal praise to reinforce the behaviors that you would like to see continue. Verbal praise looks like this. "Good job, Sam. Thanks for listening the first time and not talking back. I'm really proud of you for that."

What do you do when your child does the wrong thing?

If your child does the wrong thing and does not listen, then you need to use this chapter and the next to change his behavior. This chapter asks you to "provide options" in changing his behavior.

Before we begin to discuss how to provide options, let's cover a few important areas. First, it is essential that you remain calm, regardless of how your child tries to escalate the situation.

If he is new at exhibiting the right behavior, he is going to fight against what you are doing. He might yell or cry. This is normal. You can handle this behavior if you remain calm.

Second, behavioral change takes practice. Your child may not "get it right" the first time. You must have patience and allow him to practice the new behavior before you get frustrated at him for not getting it right.

How to Provide Options

You can't let your child get away with negative behavior. If a child does get away with bad behavior, he or she begins to learn that behavior is okay. The more your child practices negative behavior, the quicker that behavior will become his new behavior.

It is important to not let your child get away with bad behavior, but it is equally important to give him grace. I usually recommend giving kids two chances to present the right behavior before giving a negative consequence. The first time the child might blow it; he or she might totally get it wrong. By the second chance, he or she should get it right.

In between the first chance and the second chance, you PROVIDE your child OPTIONS- the chance to make the correct decision. Read the example below to see what "providing options" looks like in practice.

Mother: Bobby could you please take out the trash?
Bobby: No! I'm not taking out the trash again. It's Sam's time to take out the trash. I will not take out the trash for him again.
Mother: Bobby, I need you to understand that I am asking you to take out the trash. **You can choose to do what I ask you to do and take the trash out, or you can choose to give up your phone for three hours and go to your room. Which do you choose**? It's up to you. After you lose your phone for the three hours, I will ask you again to take out the trash and I will still expect you to do it.

At that point Bobby has a decision to make. He can choose one of the options- either to lose his phone or to do what he is asked to do. If he chooses to do the wrong thing, he is given the negative consequence, his phone is taken. If he chooses the right behavior and takes out the trash, he is given a positive consequence- lots of verbal praise.

It is important that Bobby not get out of doing what he is asked to do. Bobby must eventually take out the trash, but he might need a "cool down" period before he's re-asked to take out the trash. When he is asked to take out the trash again, he has another choice, either he can take out the trash or lose his phone for longer. Eventually his phone might be taken away for an extended period, depending on how long he refuses to obey the command. We will talk more about negative and positive consequences in the coming chapters.

In this example Bobby's mother gave Bobby a chance to make the right decision. He didn't get it right the first time. Kids usually learn quickly and begin to get it right by the second chance when they understand that there is a negative consequence that will affect them if they do not choose correctly.

Let's review one more situation of providing options. It might look like this:

Father: Gary please go brush your teeth.

Gary: (no response- ignores dad and keeps playing)

Father: Gary, this is my second time asking you to brush your teeth. You have an option, either you can go brush your teeth now, or you can lose thirty minutes of electronic time. What do you choose?

The father in this example has provided his son Gary an option after he refused to comply with the first request. Gary knows now that either he can do as he is asked or he will lose electronic time (consequence).

Think about a recent situation in which your child has not complied with an expectation. How could you re-do that situation using options to help him make a better decision?

In the next chapter we will talk about addition things that we can do to help our children make the right decision and how to change negative disruptive behaviors. For now, remember:

R- Work on relationship
E- Explain expectations
S- Break behaviors into skill sets
P- Provide options

CHAPTER SIX

*E-Encourage your child and Allow
Your Child to Make a Decision*

If your child makes the right decision, you should have skipped the information in the last chapter, and now you should skip the information in this chapter. If your child makes the right decision, give him a consequence. You can read more about consequences in the next chapter. The consequence that you give him should be a positive one. For example, if he makes the right decision the first time, praise him and give him a positive verbal consequence.

If your child does not make the right decision the first time, you should provide him options and follow up with encouragement. Using the example in the last chapter, your encouragement might look like this.

Mother: Bobby, you can choose to do what I ask you to do and take the trash out, or you can choose to give up your phone for three hours and go to your room (providing options). Which do you choose? **I know that you are going to make the right decision because you have gotten so good at listening lately (giving encouragement).**

In this example we are using a positive verbal compliment as encouragement to shape behaviors. After you provide your child with options, the second E in RESPECT is to use encouragement to help your child make the right decision. You could also say things like, "You have been doing such a great job at listening. I know you've got this." You could also say, "I have really been proud of the effort you've made lately. I am positive that you are going to make the right decision." Anything that you can say to offer encouragement to your child towards success would be helpful.

Studies show that positive reinforcement changes behaviors better than punishment. The more encouragement that you can give, the more you are better able to shape the behaviors.

What happens if this doesn't work?
What do you do if options and encouragement doesn't change the behavior and your child begins to yell, scream, or pitch a fit.

There are times when regardless of the options and positives that we give our children, they still make the wrong decision. Sometimes they escalate the situation and begin to yell, scream, and throw a tantrum. When that occurs, there are several steps to take. You will learn more about giving consequences in the next section, however, if your child begins to spiral out of control, you may try the following.

Number one, you need to extinguish the negative behavior as quickly as possible. If your child begins to "melt down," calmly say something like, "We are not going to do this behavior. I need you to stop that behavior right now." You might say, "Did you forget our rule? Can you stop the behavior, or do you need a consequence?" It is important to be quick, calm, and assertive but not to yell, threaten, or strike out.

Sometimes this will work and other times it will not. It is important for you as the parent to not engage in yelling behavior. When you yell back at your child, your child has already won. Often, a child's whole purpose is to get attention. He wants attention even if it is negative. When you yell at him, often you are reinforcing negative behavior.

If the child does not stop the negative behavior after you have requested, give your child the options. Say, "We are not going to do this behavior. You have a choice. You can either stop this behavior now, or you can lose your phone (or whatever consequence you choose) for longer. What do you choose?"

Remember when you are trying to stop negative behavior to label the behavior as negative but not the child. Never say, "you are bad." You might say, "I don't like this negative behavior," but make sure that you separate the behavior from the child.

If your child still does not stop the behavior, then you need to implement a calm down or time out period.

If your child still will not calm down, repeat again, "We are not going to have this negative behavior. You need to go take a time out to calm down. We will talk about this again when you are calm."

Calm Down or Time Out

For a small child, you might have a special chair or a safe place for him to sit to calm down. Instruct him to go to the time-out location and communicate why he is being placed in time-out. Experts agree that one to two minutes for every year of age usually works best. Time-out starts after your child quits screaming and yelling.

At times it is beneficial to put your child in time-out and not give attention to the negative behavior. Selectively ignoring the negative behavior works, but it is important to ensure that your child is safe in the time-out location.

Tell your child how long he has in time-out and inform him that his time will start after the fussing or screaming ends. If your child will not go to the time-out location on his own, you might need to take him to the location. Be sure to transport him in a calm manner and not in anger.

If you have a child that is too large to be carried, or if you have a teenager, you might have him sit on the stairs or go to his room. The place that you send him needs to be a place where there is no extra entertainment. For example, your child shouldn't go to his room and read a book. Instead, if you send him to his room, he needs to sit on his bed and not engage in activities. Be clear in your directions about what you expect and why your child is having to go to time-out. A teenager also needs 1 to 2 minutes in time-out for every year of age, although you have more flexibility at this age.

If your child is older and will not go to time-out on his own, remove yourself from the location. Say, "I am instructing you to go to time-out. Are you choosing not to go? If so, I am (give punishment) taking your phone for the rest of the day for not listening. If he continues to fuss, say, "I am not going to stay here and listen to this fussing, but I need you to understand that I am going to (give punishment) take your phone for the rest of the day due to your decision." Make sure your child is safe and begin to ignore the negative behavior by leaving the situation using selective ignoring. Remember to eventually follow through with the consequence.

You are almost through with the entire RESPECT plan. Remember:
R- work on relationship
E- explain expectations
S- break behaviors into skill sets
P- provide options
E- encourage and allow to make a decision

CHAPTER SEVEN

C-Give a Consequence

Most actions in life result in some sort of a consequence. We experience positive consequences or negative consequences after most behaviors. When we smile at others (a positive behavior), usually we receive a positive consequence back- others smile at us. When we act angry or grumpy, most of the time we receive negative consequences. For example, those around you might fuss back, ignore you, or try to avoid you.

Some sort of consequence naturally follows most behaviors; however, psychologists agree that behavior is shaped best by *positive* consequences. For example, think about your own life. Things that make you feel good motivate you to repeat the behaviors. When you are dieting, and people say, "Wow, you look great!" you are motivated to continue dieting. The more the behavior is repeated, the more the behavior is internalized and learned.

Scientists believe that dopamine, a neurotransmitter believed to stimulate the pleasure center of our brain, also acts as a motivation chemical. When dopamine is released in our brain, we repeat the activities associated. When we give our children compliments or verbal praise, we cause dopamine to be released in their brains. The dopamine causes the behavior to be repeated.

Positive consequences act on the brain to increase the correct behavior.

Kids will test the limits, but the way that we react will either reinforce or extinguish the behaviors. Our children can't see the big picture and don't always make the right choices, so it is our job to help them navigate through life by providing the right consequences to shape behaviors.

This chapter will be one of the most important chapters in this book. Consequences shape your child's behavior. If you forget the consequence, you will not be effective at behavior change. You must implement the plan in this chapter to be successful.

Remember that the behaviors of your child are separate from who he is. Also, it is *normal* for kids to test the limits. As parents we must display unconditional love, even when we dislike the negative behaviors. Since behaviors can be taught and reinforced or extinguished, you have control. Remember, the more a behavior is reinforced, the more the behavior becomes a new learned behavior. Changing your child's behavior requires action from you.

The easiest way to increase a positive behavior is to use a positive consequence; this will increase the likelihood that the behavior will occur again. When using positive consequences, it is important to remember that at times it is not important that your child get the new behavior perfectly. Psychology tells us that as your child is learning the new behaviors, it is good to reward behaviors that are *close* to the behavior that you desire. As your child gets closer to the correct behavior, you can become more exacting in your expectations.

When using both positive and negative consequences, you should reinforce with a consequence immediately after the behavior occurs. When you can't immediately reinforce, reinforce as soon as possible after the event.

Using positive reinforcement will change your child's be-havior quicker than negative reinforcement.

There are at least four types of positive consequences or reinforcement. The four types of positive consequences are: material, token, activity, and social consequences.

Four Types of Positive Consequences:

Material positive consequences are material goods that you provide your child for good behavior. To provide material consequences, you might buy them a shirt, or give them a toy.

Token positive consequences are tokens- coins, check-marks or stickers that can serve as the reward. They are "tokens" that you child can turn in for a larger reward later. Token positive consequences work well with reward charts.

Activity positive consequences are activities that you give your child for good behavior. For example, you might let them go skating, out to eat, to a ball game or any other activity that rewards them for positive behavior.

Social positive consequences are verbal words of affirmation or physical acts (hugs, pats on the arm, etc.) that you give your child after they do the right thing. Many people believe that these are the most powerful type of consequence for changing behavior. An example of a social positive consequence would be saying to your child, "You did such a great job. I am proud of you."

The more positive consequences that you can give, the quicker you will shape your child's behavior. In the chapter about relationship, we talked about 7x7x7 and giving 7 positive verbal affirmations to your child per day. Instead of the seven positive affirmations, you could also use 7 positive verbal consequences to shape your child's behavior. This would mean that any time you find your child doing the right thing, you give him or her a positive verbal consequence to cause the behavior to be repeated. For example, suppose your child puts his or her plate in the dishwasher without you asking. Then, you would say, "Thank you so much for putting the dish away without me telling you do it. You are getting so responsible." This would cause the positive behavior to be repeated.

Using Negative Consequences

The other way to change behaviors is to give a negative consequence. Again, the negative consequence should be given as quickly as possible after the incident. The consequence must be individualized, immediate, and equal to the crime.

Examples of negative consequences are time out, loss of a privilege, toy, or electronic device, or having your child do a chore instead of receiving a privilege. Negative consequences might be necessary but should be the last step after positive reinforcement fails.

Remember that the goal in behavior change is to replace the bad behavior with good behavior. If a bad behavior is allowed without a consequence, the behavior will often be repeated. It is important for you as a parent to watch your child and try to give as many positive consequences as possible to shape your child's behavior towards your family values.

Reward Charts

Reward charts are good ideas for shaping behaviors. They work well especially for children, but a modified version can be used with teens. A reward chart lists the desired behavior and usually is done weekly. At the left side, you list the behaviors that you would like to see. To the right of the chart, you list the days. A checkmark is given for the days that the behavior is exhibited. At the end of the agreed upon time frame, the child earns a reward. Usually the chart is set up weekly, however, since studies show that rewards are more effective immediately after the behavior is exhibited, a small daily reward would also be appropriate. See the example behavior chart.

Behavior	Mon	Tues	Wed	Thurs	Fri	Sat	Sun	
Susie will put dishes away without being asked								
Susie will listen without talking back								
Susie will play quietly while mom is shopping								

A check mark is given each day that Susie shows mastery of the behavior. A reward is given after Susie accumulates enough checks.

Remember:
R- work on relationship
E- explain expectations
S- break behaviors into skill sets
P- provide options
E- encourage and allow child to make decision
C- give consequences

Robin Fitzgerald

Notes:

CHAPTER EIGHT

T- Train again

Part of being human is that we are not perfect, and we make lots of mistakes. When I make a mistake I like to be forgiven. In addition, I like for people to remember the good parts about me and focus less on my mistakes. How about you?

Our children are the same way. Part of RESPECT parenting is demonstrating respect. Not only do we want our children to respect us, but we must respect them.

My mom was a teacher for 35 years. She passed away several years ago, but her students still come up to me and tell me how much she meant to them. Mom attributed her success as a teacher to respect. She would always say, "If you respect students, they will respect you."

The same is true of our own kids. As they learn to be adults they will mess up a lot. Honestly, I am still messing up- even at my age. When I mess up, I desire that people respect me enough to give me grace.

Part of demonstrating grace is knowing that you might have to train your child on the same thing over and over and over again. If your child messes up, it is necessary to go through the same process of behavioral interventions until he or she can achieve positive behaviors.

Remember, your child is worth the effort! The T in RESPECT is TRAIN again.

Remember, there WILL be times when you will have to retrain!

Accept the fact that at times you will have to re-train. Often kids will not achieve the desired behavior the first time. Depending on your child, you might have to retrain again and again. Eventually, with patience, however, your child will "get it!"

During the re-training process, remember that your children will become what you tell them. In psychology, we call this a self-fulfilling prophecy.

There are lots of interesting new studies about beliefs. There is evidence that if people believe something, the belief will often come true.

Recently I read a story about a person who was told that he had cancer and three weeks to live. The person died in three weeks just as the doctor predicted. When the hospital did an autopsy on the person, however, they found the doctor had been wrong. The man did not have cancer; he had actually been well. The man died not because he was sick but because he *believed* that he was sick.

Our beliefs affect us greatly. There are many studies that demonstrate how placebo drugs help cure, how average students excel when they believe that they are special, and even how medical issues resolve when people believe correctly.

Let your child become a self-fulfilling prophecy. You must fill your child's mind with positives: tell your son how special he is; tell your daughter that God has a great plan for her life that only she can accomplish; tell your son how brilliant he is; tell your daughter that she is an awesome child.

By faith, speak into your child's life what you would like to materialize. The Bible tells us in Proverbs 18:21 that the power of life and death is in our tongue. Speak the words of life over your children's destiny.

Remember:

R- work on relationship
E- explain expectations
S- break behaviors into skill sets
P- provide options
E- encourage and allow child to make decision
C- give consequences
T- train again

Robin Fitzgerald

Notes:

CHAPTER NINE

Final Thoughts

I hate to say this, but sometimes we must remember to lower our expectations! We want our children to behave appropriately, but we must consider that they are still kids. Scientists are now saying that a person's brain is not fully developed until he is around 25-years-old. This means that it is unrealistic to expect kids to make adult decisions. Behavioral change takes time and work.

Both children and teenagers need a few basic things. They need praise and affection. They also need for us to foster in them a sense of independence and an ability to do things for themselves. They need love and guidance.

As a child moves into his teenage years, it is normal for his behavior to change. It is very possible that your child moves from an obedient child to a moody new person that sometimes seems like a stranger.

As parents, it is our job to help our children navigate the journey from child to adult. This includes planning ahead, especially in teenage years, for risky situations that they may encounter during their journey of growth. It is a good idea to discuss with your teen potential risky situations that he or she might encounter and how to successfully conquer the obstacles.

The need for socialization also increases as a child moves into the teenage years. As a parent, it is important that you help provide socialization activities- opportunities for your child to interact with other teens in a positive manner. Your teen needs the freedom to become independent and help finding his or her "niche" - a place to "fit" that is positive and where your child can feel good. Remember that having positive activities helps reduce the likelihood that your child will choose negative or deviant activities. It is very important that you, as the parent, work to cultivate opportunities for him or her to fit in and feel good.

Behavioral contracts with teens are good ideas. You might consider a cell phone contract, a driving contract, or a contract that ensures that they will call you if they encounter a risky situation.

In summary, behavioral change takes work, but the benefits are worth the effort. Remember the word RESPECT.

R- work on relationship
E- explain expectations
S- break behaviors into skill sets
P- provide options
E- encourage and allow child to make decision
C- give consequences
T- train again

Summary

Parenting is one of the hardest jobs that you will ever be given, but, you have the tools that you need to navigate this process. Remember that God loves not just your child, but you too. Take time for yourself. Make sure that you work through any issues from childhood that might be holding you back. Focus on happiness pegs throughout your day. Plan into your day things that make you feel good like a special cup of coffee or an evening out with someone you love.

It is much easier to parent when YOUR love tank is full, and you feel good about life. If you don't take time for yourself, you will not be an effective parent. Your happiness begins with you!

I pray for you that God equips you to do mighty things for his kingdom and that your lineage will follow. I pray that your child begins to listen, and you experience how wonderful it is to have a family that moves in harmony. I pray mostly that you know the height and depth of God's love for you and how important you are to him.

Thanks for sharing this time with me!

Be blessed!

Robin

Robin Fitzgerald

References

Change Your Thoughts, Change Your Life. David Stoop, Revell, Grand Rapids, Michigan.

https://mentalhealthdaily.com/2015/02/18/at-**what-age**-is-the-**brain**...